The Illustrators of Alice

K.M. Roberts. S.W. Partridge, London 1908.

THE ILLUSTRATORS OF
ALICE IN WONDERLAND
AND
THROUGH THE LOOKING GLASS

edited by
Graham Ovenden

with an introduction by
John Davis

ACADEMY EDITIONS   LONDON
ST. MARTIN'S PRESS   NEW YORK

ACKNOWLEDGEMENTS

We should like to thank the many publishers who have given us permission to reproduce illustrations; and the following people for their assistance in compiling the list of illustrators and providing information on books in their collections: June Moll of the University of Texas, Stanley Marx, Peter Blake and Selwyn Goodacre (who also helped to revise material for this new edition). We are also grateful to Denis Crutch, Edward Guillano and the many others who helped in revising the text and supplying additional information.

Page 1:
Mervyn Peake, 1946.

Opposite:
Millicent Sowerby. Chatto & Windus, London 1907.

Published in Great Britain by
Academy Editions 7 Holland Street London W8

First edition 1972. Revised edition 1979.
Copyright © 1972, 1979 Academy Editions
All rights reserved

Published in the USA by
St. Martin's Press Inc
175 Fifth Avenue New York NY 10010
ISBN: 0-312-408463
Library of Congress Catalog Card Number: 79-5355

Printed and bound in Great Britain by
Hazell Watson & Viney Ltd, Aylesbury

Well over a hundred artists have illustrated Lewis Carroll's *Alice's Adventures in Wonderland* and *Through the Looking-Glass and What Alice Found There* since they were first published in 1865 and 1871. Clearly these books have fascinated artists in the same way as they have appealed to readers. The treatment of Carroll's characters has varied from the surrealistic to the mundane: contemporary events and attitudes are frequently reflected - the cost of the Mad Hatter's hat fluctuating with current prices, the Playing Cards wearing Prussian helmets in pre-1914 illustrations, demarcation-conscious Trade Unionists disputing over the painted rose tree in 1957. But in outlining the approach that a number of artists have taken, any order of merit is purely subjective. From the many illustrations reproduced, the reader can make his own judgement.

To discuss Alice's illustrations without discussing Alice's creator would be impossible. Charles Lutwidge Dodgson, the son of the Rector of Daresbury in Cheshire, was born on January 27th, 1832. He was educated at Richmond, Yorkshire, and Rugby and in 1851 came into residence at Christ Church, Oxford, with which he was to be associated for the rest of his life; inevitably college life and politics are closely woven into much of his writing. In 1854 he graduated and in 1855 was appointed Sub-Librarian of Christ Church. By the end of the year he became in his own words 'master and tutor in Ch.Ch., with an income of more than £300 a year and the course of mathematical tuition marked out by God's providence for at least some years to come.' He was ordained deacon in 1861 but never proceeded to priest's orders.

From 1845 onwards Charles Dodgson wrote prose and poems for a number of public and private magazines and in 1856 Lewis Carroll was born, although, at the time, nobody recognised him. In that year, when writing for *The Train,* he felt the need of a pseudonym and proposed a number of alternatives to the magazine's editor, Edmund Yates. The first suggested names were typical of his mental processes - Edgar Cuthwellis or Edgar U.C. Westhill, anagrams of his christian names Charles Lutwidge. The second two proposals were Louis Carroll or Lewis Carroll, variants of Charles, Carolus, Carroll and Lutwidge, Ludovicus, Lewis. Edmund Yates chose Lewis Carroll and from the publication of the poem *Solitude* in March 1856, this became Dodgson's *nom de plume* for his non-academic writings, Dodgson being retained for his serious publications.

On July 4th, 1862 there was a very important entry in Carroll's diary, 'I made an expedition up the river to Godstow with the three Liddells; we had tea on the bank there, and did not reach Christ Church again till half past eight.' This short sentence describes the first telling of *Alice's Adventures in Wonderland* to Alice, Lorina and Edith Liddell, the three daughters of Dean Liddell of Christ Church. On Carroll's return to Oxford that evening he promised to write out his story but it was some time before that promise was fulfilled. By January 1863 the manuscript was completed and illustrated with some of Carroll's pen and ink sketches. It was shown to Henry Kingsley, the brother of the author of *The Water Babies,* who urged Carroll to publish it since he immediately recognised its merit. Other friends, including George Macdonald, were approached for comments and again enthusiastic responses were received. Over the next one and a half years Carroll rewrote his story but realising his lack of skill as an artist, he looked about for a professional illustrator. In February 1864, following an introduction from Tom Taylor, he approached John Tenniel who had already illustrated several children's books including *Undine* and *Aesop's Fables.* Tenniel seems to have taken some months to consider the proposal but final agreement was reached in April.

Tenniel was a mild and gentle man but his relationship with Carroll was stormy though mutually concealed beneath a veneer of Victorian politeness. Carroll is said to have told Harry Furniss that he had not liked any of Tenniel's drawings except Humpty Dumpty! The original child of Carroll's story was Alice Liddell but Tenniel's illustrations were undoubtedly based on Mary Hilton Badcock, a photograph of whom Carroll sent to Tenniel with the suggestion that she might make a good model. Tenniel probably worked straight from the photograph as he rarely used live models. His illustrations for *Alice's Adventures in Wonderland* are a perfect example of the combination between artist and author and to many they are inseparable. Perhaps Tenniel's weakness, if any be admitted, is in his drawings of Alice herself who frequently appears overly serious and expressionless. But he must be placed unequivocally as one, if not the greatest, of the many illustrators of Alice.

When Tenniel had finished the drawings, Carroll persuaded Macmillan, publishers to Oxford University, to undertake publication of *Alice's Adventures in Wonderland* on a commission basis. In July 1865 the first edition was issued. Two weeks after publication, Tenniel told Carroll that he was dissatisfied with the reproduction of the illustrations and Carrol

A.L. Bowley, 1921.

Lewis Carroll, 1886.

called in as many as he could of the fifty or so copies that had either been sold or given away to his child friends. A second edition, the type reset and printed by Richard Clay, was published in November 1865 but dated 1866. The unbound sheets of the first edition were not scrapped but sold to America where they were bound up with a new frontispiece and issued in 1866.

Carroll was now achieving international fame from his book and translations, with the Tenniel illustrations, appeared in French, German and Italian, whilst several editions were published in the U.S.A. Within a year, he had decided upon a sequel but determined to find a suitable artist first. His initial approach to Tenniel, who had found Carroll very fussy to work with, was rejected. Carroll then approached a number of other artists, including Richard Doyle and Sir Noel Paton, even considering W.S. Gilbert, but all politely refused. Tenniel eventually accepted only after Carroll's renewed pleading. The successful team was thus reunited to quarrel and bicker once more but, perhaps, in *Through the Looking-Glass and What Alice Found There,* to present a more impressive and a more united book.

Tenniel's reputation had also been enhanced by his *Wonderland* illustrations, and he appears to have taken a stronger and even more forceful line with this second book. Carroll continued to maintain his independence advising, 'Don't give Alice so much crinoline' and 'The White Knight must not have whiskers', but Tenniel's knight was whiskered and old and, reputedly, bore a striking resemblance to one of his colleagues in *Punch,* a certain Ponny Mayhew. Tenniel also managed to convince Carroll to shorten his book from thirteen chapters to twelve following correspondence containing such remarks as 'Don't think me brutal, but I am bound to say that the *'wasp'* chapter doesn't interest me in the least and

Willy Pogany, 1929.

Philip Gough, 1949.

I can't see my way to a picture. If you want to shorten the book, I can't help thinking - with all submission - that here is your opportunity.' He also remarked that a 'wasp in a wig is beyond the appliance of art'. In 1974 the galley proof for this supressed 'Wasp in a Wig' chapter of *Through the Looking-Glass* was auctioned at Sotheby's, London and subsequently the text was published in London and New York in 1977. *Through the Looking-Glass and What Alice Found There* was published in time for Christmas 1871, though the first edition was dated 1872. It was an immediate success and like *Alice's Adventures in Wonderland* has been re-printed many times.

Once again Tenniel had excelled himself with fifty illustrations compared with the forty-two in *Wonderland*. Again his mastery of animals and humans was apparent and in this book his drawings of Alice seem softer and less wooden; his interpretation and technique both superb, his Jabberwock is suitably fearsome whilst the frontispiece of the White Knight seems to have an echo of Durer in both composition and print quality. It is interesting, too, that the pictures of Alice entering and emerging from the looking-glass appear on consecutive pages, as if her entry into wonderland was happening in the book itself. The combination of artist and writer seems more satisfying in this than in the preceding work and is perhaps best described in the words of one of Tenniel's biographers who said that there may be better drawings but no better illustrations.

Before examining the rest of Alice's illustrators, the one to be considered first must be Lewis Carroll himself. Indeed he should be regarded as the first illustrator of *Alice in Wonderland* as his original manuscript for Alice Liddell included many of his own sketches. However, his confidence in his own artistic ability must have been sapped when Ruskin remarked that he had not enough talent to make it worth his while to devote much time to

Charles Robinson, 1907.   **Sir John Tenniel**, 1872.

sketching. Carroll did not possess the technical expertise of Tenniel but he did try to represent the characters that he had created. As the central character Alice appears in twenty-seven of the thirty-seven illustrations whilst Tenniel only pictured her twenty-three times in his forty-two pictures. Carroll's Alice is a serious-minded little girl quite capable of coping with the illogical wonderland. It is understandable that these drawings lacked appeal to the upper middle class children's readership of the nineteenth century whose taste was largely dictated by their parents. However, Carroll's drawings warrant reassessment now that technical accuracy in presentation is no longer held in such high esteem. In their way they have a soul which is lacking in those of Tenniel and are much more moving. Carroll arranged for the text and pictures to be published in 1886 under the title of *Alice's Adventures Under Ground*. This was not a success and only one edition was printed in Carroll's lifetime.

Whilst Carroll was alive, few artists had either the wish or the opportunity to compete with Tenniel's illustrations. In 1880 Kate Freiligarth-Kroeker's *Alice and Other Fairy Plays* was published with several uninteresting illustrations by Mary Sibree and this was followed in 1882 by an even worse frontispiece of the Tweedles to *Alice Through the Looking-Glass and Other Fairy Plays for Children* by the same author. In 1884, Stanley Leathes produced *Alice's Wonderland Birthday Book* which

Mervyn Peake, 1946.   **Harry Furniss**, 1909.

contained a number of illustrations by J.P.M. There is a Carroll quotation
for each day, facing pages arranged for birthday entries. All three books
were produced with Carroll's full permission and are unusual mainly
because he allowed an artist other than Tenniel to illustrate his stories. In
1896, some two years before Carroll's death in 1898, Blanche McManus
illustrated an American edition of *Alice in Wonderland*. There seems to be
no record of any comments by Carroll on these drawings which are
pleasant but undistinguished.

The flood of illustrated editions of *Alice in Wonderland* started shortly
after Carroll's death, first in the United States, then in Britain. Between
1899 and 1904 four further American editions were published, of which the
best-known was that of Peter Newell. Newell produced forty pictures for
an elegantly designed edition, the text surrounded with beautiful
ornamental designs, but the drawings having a flat theatrical quality with
neither the simplicity to endear them to children nor the perception to

A.E. Jackson, 1915.   **A.L. Bowley**, 1921.

appeal to adults and in no way rivalling the humour and the draughtsmanship of Tenniel. In 1907 the British copyright in *Alice in Wonderland* expired and there was an almost indecent rush by publishers to produce editions with new illustrations; at least eight being published in the autumn of that year.

The first, issued in October, was the Chatto and Windus edition with coloured drawings by Millicent Sowerby. Despite an unusual title page, the pictures are uninspired, though pleasing, and the whole production disappointing considering that one had been waiting for forty years for a successor to Tenniel.

The next edition, published towards the end of 1907, was illustrated by Thomas Maybank, and memorable more for its production so soon after the expiration of the copyright than for an individual pictorial interpretation of the text. This was followed by that of Arthur Rackham, already well known as an illustrator of children's books before he tackled Alice and he must be regarded as the first artist to bear comparison to Tenniel. His watercolours are magnificent with a haunting quality; browns and greys predominating in his compositions. He excels in backgrounds of gnarled trees with mischievous eyes, which occasionally dominate the characters. His Alice is maturer than Tenniel's, whilst his Mad Hatter has a sharper East End quality and, in fact, has reduced the price of his hat from 10/6 to 8/11.

Also in November, 1907, came an edition with eight coloured plates and one hundred and twelve other illustrations by Charles Robinson. The Robinson brothers were talented artists; Charles and Thomas Heath both illustrated *Alice in Wonderland,* although the task was not undertaken by their more famous brother William Heath, the humorous contributor to

11

Sir John Tenniel, 1865.   **Willy Pogany**, 1929.

Punch. Charles's illustrations are quite delightful and amongst the many there must be some to suit all tastes. His picture of Alice creating the Pool of Tears thoroughly captures the particular passage in the text, whilst that of the Frog Footman or the Gryphon are typical of the individual sketches scattered throughout the book. Scarcely a page passes without an illustration which is, after all, how a children's book should be presented, particularly in 1907. Charles Robinson's pictures are memorable and it seems a pity that this edition does not seem to have been reprinted since 1928.

Of the eight illustrated editions of *Alice in Wonderland* issued in 1907, those by Arthur Rackham and Charles Robinson appear to be the only two which captured the story in a new but memorable style. Alice Ross's pictures are slight and clearly based on Tenniel; W.H. Walker draws a graceful Alice, particularly as she rises out of the Pool of Tears, and his Mad Hatter has slashed the price to 3/6 for a curious bowler hat. His is a straight-forward, competent set of illustrations, blending well with the story.

From 1908 onwards new illustrators tackled *Alice in Wonderland* almost every year. Each obviously contributed his own style and expertise but few produced a really original approach and many seemed prosaic in performance as if under instructions from their publisher to illustrate

Charles Robinson, 1907.   **Robert Högfeldt,** 1945.

Lewis Carroll's book after *Robinson Crusoe* and before *Grimm's Fairy Tales.* The New Zealander Harry Rountree (1908) was another of the *Punch* artists to tackle Alice. His animals are good though perhaps a little fussy, but the human characters lack conviction. A.E. Jackson (1915) produced a series of pleasantly coloured illustrations with a more contemporary Alice, a splendid Mad Hatter and a beautifully coiffeured un-ugly Duchess.

Charles Robinson's brother, Thomas Heath Robinson, jointly illustrated *Alice in Wonderland* with Charles Pears. This is interesting as it is rare for two artists to undertake such a task and, to be honest, there seems to have been little if any collaboration between the two illustrators: Alice, the Mad Hatter and the March Hare are each interpreted in completely different ways. Pears merely redraws Tenniel's pictures in colour whilst Thomas Heath produces a set of charming illustrations. His interpretation of the meeting between Alice, who throughout these pictures is more mature than is customary, and the Pigeon is exquisite. One wonders at the reason for this joint production as alone Thomas Heath Robinson could have created a book comparable to but different from that of his brother Charles.

One artist stands out during the rather barren wilderness of the 20s and 30s - Willy Pogany (1929). His Art Deco illustrations have an altogether

Lewis Carroll, 1886.   **A.L. Bowley**, 1921.

new, crisp, clean style, the first really original interpretation since Tenniel
and a milestone in the artistic characterisation of Alice. Alice is a 30s
American bobbysoxer with a page boy hairstyle and the Mad Hatter is
definitely a member of the rag trade. Of the playing cards, the clubs appear
as West Point cadets, the diamonds and hearts straight from the Ziegfield
Follies chorus line, whilst the spades are obviously members of the
painters' and decoractors' union. D.R. Sexton (1933) also produced a 30s
Alice with lipstick and eye shadow but sadly lacking the depth of Pogany's
reinterpretation.

Of contemporary artists who have illustrated *Wonderland* Ralph
Steadman (1967) has produced a series of pictures in a style probably
appealing only to adults, totally different from that of any predecessor.
His comparisons between Carroll characters and present day equivalents are
astute and although his drawings may not attract all Alice lovers, he must
be recognised as the first artist to attempt a radical reinterpretation.
Salvador Dali's series of lithographs for a magnificent limited edition
(1969), which unfortunately proved technically impossible to reproduce in
this selection, is pure surrealism. Alice, with a skipping rope, recurs in all
the drawings; the table top upon which the Mad Hatter's tea party is held is
formed from one of Dali's melting watches, and, in another picture,
Alice's hand protrudes from a typical Mediterranean villa. Max Ernst
(1970) illustrated the Mad Hatter's tea party in *Lewis Carroll's
Wunderhorn,* a selection of Carroll's logic and letters, in a lithograph

Charles Robinson, 1907.   **Margaret Tarrant,** 1916.

where words are compressed in a mathematical pattern.Graham Ovenden, whose complete Alice paintings and screen-prints have not yet been published in book form, has taken a unique and personal approach: in all his illustrations only Alice is depicted. In every case, her reaction to a particular situation is emphasised. Drawn with immense sensitivity and depth of feeling for Carroll's story, they have a timeless quality that must appeal even to the purists amongst Alice lovers.

Alice in Wonderland has surely been illustrated by more artists than any other children's book; one is tempted to say than any other fictional work. But *Through the Looking-Glass* does not seem to have had the same appeal. Several artists have illustrated both volumes, only a mere four seem to have tackled *Looking-Glass* alone: Franklin Hughes, Nan Fullerton, Bridgeman and Peter Blake. The majority of publishers seem to have been content to reprint Tenniel's illustrations.

The first British edition with new illustrations, by Harry Rountree, was published in 1928. Again, his animal characters are the best feature. But in the United States there were several earlier editions. Blanche McManus (1899) was again the first, with a set of illustrations that repeat the limitations of those she designed for *Wonderland*. Peter Newell's *Through the Looking-Glass* (1901) is more successful, the pictures more in tune with the text than those he did for *Wonderland,* but the round faced oriental chess pieces pall and the glossy photographic reproductions of his drawings become tedious. It was not until the 30s onwards, both in

Sir John Tenniel, 1865.   **Arthur Rackham,** 1907.

England and America, that some really distinguished illustrations were produced.

Of these a set of elegant watercolours by the American artist Franklin Hughes (1931) combines the rather flat geometric style of much of American art of the 30s with a curiously contemporary quality. In England, Edgar Thurstan produced a striking set of pictures at about the same time. His Alice is more mature than in many other portrayals, although not as surprisingly adult as J. Morton Sale's, and his Humpty Dumpty reminds one of an insecure business executive just about to fall off his chair. Indeed, in both this and the next decade some of the most interesting editions were published. Philip Gough set both books in a delightful rococo background, his Tweedledum and Tweedledee depicted as minor French courtiers. The Scandinavian Robert Högfeldt (1945), one of the few foreign artists whose pictures were published in an English-language edition, produced a series of splendid animals - particularly the Mock Turtle, whose sadness pervades the page.

But perhaps the most memorable interpretation comes from Mervyn Peake (1954) of whose illustrations Graham Greene wrote 'You are the first person who has been able to illustrate the book satisfactorily since Tenniel, though I still argue as I think I argued with you years ago that your Alice is a little bit too much of a gamin.' This gamin quality of Alice is set against the weird, almost macabre, drawings of the other characters such as the Mad Hatter. In common with several artists who illustrated both books, Peake's drawings are even more successful in *Through the*

16

Above: **Maraja,** 1959.

Right:
'Alice took up the fan and gloves, and, as
the hall was very hot, she kept fanning
herself all the time she went on talking,'
Mabel Lucie Attwell, 1910.

Looking-Glass than *Wonderland.* In 1970 Peter Blake produced a superb series of watercolours based on *Through the Looking-Glass* and it is interesting to see the work of an artist, rather than an illustrator, who has been inspired by this book.

Inevitably, Tenniel's illustrations have deeply influenced the work of nearly all the other artists who have approached *Alice in Wonderland* and *Through the Looking-Glass.* This is understandable as the various characters are meticulously described by Carroll, who left little scope for the artist to do much more than embellish the story. This introduction has only sketched out the history of the writing and publication of the two books and summarised the work of certain artists. A detailed analysis would need a much lengthier study but for those interested in further reading on the subject, a short bibliography of works on Carroll and one of illustrated English language editions have been included (pages 84-87).

It would be naive to regard this list as comprehensive but it contains more entries than any previously published. No attempt has been made to list artists who have illustrated foreign language editions, although some pictures from such editions have been selected.

Have any artists succeeded in meeting the challenge of Tenniel? Pride of place amongst other illustrators must go to Lewis Carroll himself, Rackham, Pogany, Peake, Steadman, Dali, Ernst, Blake and Ovenden, but another lover of the Alice books could, and probably would, create a totally different list.

Below:
Willy Pogany, 1929.

ALICE'S ADVENTURES IN WONDERLAND

Millicent Sowerby. Title page from the Chatto & Windus edition, London 1907.

Chapter 1
DOWN THE RABBIT-HOLE

Above:
'but, when the Rabbit actually *took a watch out of its waistcoat-pocket,* and looked at it. . .'
A.L. Bowley. Raphael Tuck, London 1921.

Right:
Helen Munro. Nelson Famous Books, London 1932.

Chapter 2
The Pool of Tears

'Poor Alice! It was as much as she could do, lying down on one side, to look through into the garden with one eye; but to get through was more hopeless than ever: she sat down and began to cry again.'
Thomas Maybank. G. Routledge, London 1907.

'It was high time to go, for the pool was getting quite crowded with the birds and animals that had fallen into it: there was a Duck and a Dodo, a Lory and an Eaglet, and several other curious creatures.'
W.H. Walker. John Lane, London 1907.

' "You ought to be ashamed of yourself," said Alice, "a great girl like you," (she might well say this), "to go on crying in this way! Stop this moment, I tell you!" But she went on all the same, shedding gallons of tears, until there was a large pool all around her,'
Charles Robinson. Cassell, London 1907.

Chapter 3
A Caucus-race and a Long Tale

Philip Gough. The Heirloom Library, London 1949.

'At last the Mouse, who seemed to be a person of some authority among them, called out "Sit down, all of you, and listen to me! *I'll* soon make you dry enough!" They all sat down at once, in a large ring, with the Mouse in the middle.'
Sir John Tenniel. Macmillan, London 1865.

' "William the Conqueror, whose cause was favoured by the pope, was soon submitted to by the English, who wanted leaders, and had been of late much accustomed to usurpation and conquest. Edwin and Morcar, the earls of Mercia and Northumbria . . . declared for him:" '
Franz Haacken. George Bitter Verlag, Berlin 1970.

25

Chapter 4
THE RABBIT SENDS IN A LITTLE BILL

Rene Cloke. P.R. Gawthorn, London 1943.

'Still she went on growing, and, as a last resource she put one arm out of the window, and one foot up the chimney,'
Sir John Tenniel. Macmillan, London 1865.

'She went on growing and growing, and very soon had to kneel down on the floor: in another minute there was not even room for this, and she tried the effect of lying down with one elbow against the door, and the other arm curled round her head.'
Lewis Carroll. *Alice's Adventures Under Ground.* Macmillan, London 1886.

'after waiting till she fancied she heard the Rabbit just under the window, she suddenly spread out her hand, and made a snatch in the air. She did not get hold of anything, but she heard a little shriek and a fall, and a crash of broken glass . . .'
Charles Robinson. Cassell, London 1907.

Chapter 5
ADVICE FROM A CATERPILLAR

"You are old," said the youth, "as I mentioned before,
And have grown most uncommonly fat;
Yet you turned a back-somersault in at the door -
Pray, what is the reason of that?"

Phillip Gough. The Heirloom Library, London 1949.

Above:
' "three inches is such a wretched height to be." "It is a very good height indeed!" said the Caterpillar angrily,'
Harry Rountree. Nelson, London 1908.

Above left:
'The next moment she felt a violent blow underneath her chin: it had struck her foot!'
D.R. Sexton. J.F. Shaw, London 1933.

Left:
'all she could see, when she looked down, was an immense length of neck, which seemed to rise like a stalk out of a sea of green leaves that lay far below her.'
Thomas Heath Robinson. William Collins, London 1921.

' ''Serpent!'' screamed the Pigeon. ''I'm *not* a serpent!'' said Alice indignantly. ''Let me alone!'' '
Arthur Rackham. William Heinemann, London 1907.

Chapter 6
PIG AND PEPPER

" — or next day, maybe,"
the Footman continued, exactly
as if nothing had happened

' "I shall sit here," the Footman remarked, "till tomorrow -" At this moment the door of the house opened, and a large plate came skimming out, straight at the Footman's head: it just grazed his nose, and broke to pieces against one of the trees behind him. "- or next day maybe," the Footman continued in the same tone, exactly as if nothing had happened.'
Thomas Maybank. G. Routledge, London 1907.

'As soon as she had made out the proper way of nursing it. . . she carried it out into the open air.'
Robert Högfeldt. Jan Forlag, Stockholm 1945.

'the Fish Footman was gone, and the other was sitting on the ground near the door, staring stupidly up into the sky.'
Charles Robinson. Cassell, London 1907.

'The door led right into a large kitchen, which was full of smoke from one end to the other: the Duchess was sitting on a three-legged stool in the middle, nursing a baby: the cook was leaning over the fire, stirring a large cauldron which seemed to be full of soup.'
Willy Pogany. E.P. Dutton, New York 1929.

Chapter 7
A Mad Tea-Party

'the last time she saw them, they were trying to put the Dormouse into the teapot.'
Harry Rountree. Nelson, London 1908.

Right:
Mervyn Peake. Zephyr Books, Stockholm 1946.

Blanche McManus. Mansfield, New York 1896.

'This piece of rudeness was more than Alice could bear: she got up in great disgust, and walked off: the Dormouse fell asleep instantly, and neither of the others took the least notice of her going, though she looked back once or twice, half hoping that they would call after her:'
Graham Ovenden. Pencil, 1969.

Chapter 8
THE QUEEN'S CROQUET-GROUND

' "Look out now, Five! Don't go splashing paint over me like that!" "I couldn't help it," said Five, in a sulky tone. "Seven jogged my elbow." On which Seven looked up and said "That's right, Five! Always lay the blame on others!" "*You'd* better not talk!" said Five. "I heard the Queen say only yesterday you deserved to be beheaded." "What for?" said the one who had spoken first. "That's none of *your* business, Two!" said Seven. "Yes, it *is* his business!" said Five.'

Ralph Steadman. Dennis Dobson, London 1967.

' "You sha'n't be beheaded!" said Alice, and she put them into a large flower-pot that stood near.'
W.H. Walker. John Lane, London 1907.

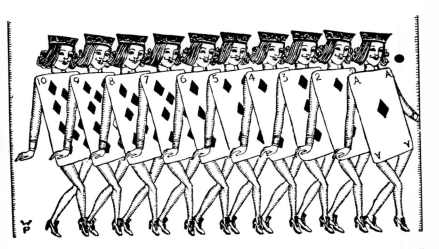

'First came ten soldiers carrying clubs, . . . next the ten courtiers: these were ornamented all over with diamonds, and walked two and two, as the soldiers did.'
Willy Pogany. E.P. Dutton, New York 1929.

'The chief difficulty Alice found at first was in managing her flamingo: she succeeded in getting its body tucked away, comfortably enough, under her arm, with its legs hanging down, but generally, just as she had got its neck nicely straightened out, and was going to give the hedgehog a blow with its head, it *would* twist itself round and look up in her face,' **Fritz Haaken**. George Bitter Verlag, Berlin 1968.

40

Chapter 9
THE MOCK TURTLE'S STORY

'The Gryphon sat up and rubbed its eyes: then it watched the Queen till she was out of sight: then it chuckled. ''What fun!'' said the Gryphon, half to itself, half to Alice.'
Charles Robinson. Cassell, London 1907.

'They had not gone far before they saw the Mock Turtle in the distance, sitting sad and lonely on a little ledge of rock, and, as they came nearer, Alice could hear him sighing as if his heart would break.
Robert Högfeldt. Jan Forlag, Stockholm 1945.

' "You can't think how glad I am to see you again, you dear old thing!" said the Duchess, as she tucked her arm affectionately into Alice's, and they walked off together.'
Thomas Heath Robinson. William Collins, London 1922.

Chapter 10
THE LOBSTER QUADRILLE

'So they began solemnly dancing round and round Alice, every now and then treading on her toes when they passed too close, and waving their fore-paws to mark the time,'
Sir John Tenniel. Macmillan, London 1866.

' "What trial is it?" Alice panted as she ran; but the Gryphon answered "Come on!" and ran the faster,'
Willy Pogany. E.P. Dutton, New York 1929.

' "Come on!" cried the Gryphon, and, taking Alice by the hand, it hurried off, without waiting for the end of the song.'
Millicent Sowerby. Chatto & Windus, London 1907.

Chapter 11
WHO STOLE THE TARTS?

Thomas Maybank, 1907.

W.H. Walker, 1907.

' ''I can't help it,'' said Alice very meekly; ''I'm growing.'' '
Willy Pogany. E.P. Dutton, New York 1929.

'Here the Queen put on her spectacles, and began staring hard at the Hatter, who turned pale and fidgeted. "Give your evidence," said the King; "and don't be nervous, or I'll have you executed on the spot."'

Harry Furniss. *The World's Great Books,* Hammerton, London 1909.

'The next witness was the Duchess's cook. She carried the pepper-box in her hand, and Alice guessed who it was, even before she got into the court, by the way the people near the door began sneezing all at once.'
K.M. Roberts. S.W. Partridge, London 1908.

Chapter 12
ALICE'S EVIDENCE

'and she jumped up in such a hurry that she tipped over the jury-box with the edge of her skirt upsetting all the jury-men on to the heads of the crowd below,'
A.E. Jackson. Henry Frowde, London 1915.

Peter Blake. Watercolour for screenprint, 1970.

Graham Ovenden. Oil on paper, 1969.

Max Ernst. Lithograph from *Lewis Carroll's Wunderhorn,* Stuttgart 1970.

Bessie Pease Gutmann. *Alice's Adventures in Wonderland,* London 1908.

Arthur Rackham. *Alice's Adventures in Wonderland,* London 1907.

The Wonderland Quadrille. Music cover. Chromo lithograph after Tenniel, c. 1872-5.

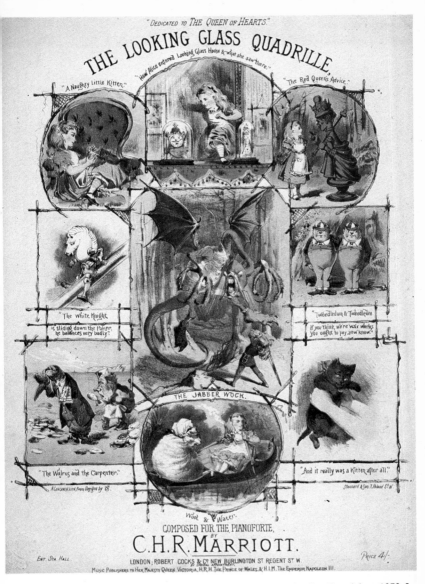

The Looking-Glass Quadrille. Music cover. Chromo lithograph after Tenniel, c. 1872-5.

Charles Robinson. *Alice's Adventures in Wonderland*, London 1907.

' "Oh, I've had such a curious dream!" said Alice. And she told her sister, as well as she could remember them, all these strange Adventures of hers,'
W.H. Walker. John Lane, 1907.

Through the Looking-glass
and
What Alice Found There

ALICE & DINAH

Chapter 1
LOOKING-GLASS HOUSE

Above left:
'In another moment Alice was through the glass, and had jumped down lightly into the Looking-glass room.'
Sir John Tenniel. Macmillan, London 1872.

Above right:
'The King immediately fell flat on his back, and lay perfectly still; and Alice was a little alarmed at what she had done, and went round the room to see if she could find any water to throw over him. However, she could find nothing but a bottle of ink, and when she got back with it she found he had recovered, and he and the Queen were talking together in a frightened whisper -'
J. Morton Sale. William Clowes, London 1933.

Left:
Gwynedd M. Hudson. Hodder & Stoughton, London 1922.

Chapter 2
THE GARDEN OF LIVE FLOWERS

'She had not been walking a minute before she found herself face to face with the Red Queen, and full in sight of the hill she had been so long aiming at.'
Franklin Hughes. Cheshire House, New York 1931.

' ''Where do you come from?'' said the Red Queen. ''And where are you going? Look up, speak nicely, and don't twiddle your fingers all the time.'' Alice attended to all these directions, and explained, as well as she could, that she had lost her way.'
Peter Newell. Harper, New York 1902.

Chapter 3

LOOKING-GLASS INSECTS

'All this time the Guard was looking at her, first through a telescope, then through a microscope, and then through an opera-glass. At last he said "You're travelling the wrong way," and shut up the window, and went away.'
Sir John Tenniel. Macmillan, London 1872.

The Bread-and-butter-fly.

The Rocking-horse-fly.

The Snap-dragon-fly.

Left:
'this was anything but a regular bee: in fact, it was an elephant - as Alice soon found out, though the idea quite took her breath away at first. ''And what enormous flowers they must be!'' was her next idea. ''Something like cottages with the roofs taken off, and stalks put to them -'' '
Robert Högfeldt. Jan Forlag, Stockholm, 1945.

Chapter 4
Tweedledum and Tweedledee

Philip Gough. The Heirloom Library, London 1949.

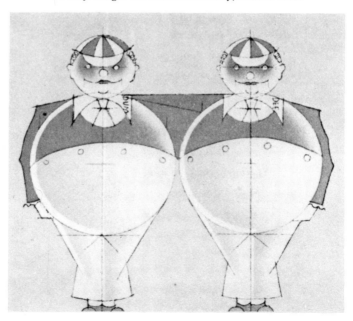

Peter Blake. Screenprint, 1970.

Left:
'They were standing under a tree, each with an arm round the other's neck, and Alice knew which was which in a moment, because one of them had 'DUM' embroidered on his collar, and the other 'DEE'. "I suppose they've each got 'TWEEDLE' round at the back of the collar," she said to herself.'
Franklin Hughes. Cheshire House, New York 1931.

' "The sun was shining on the sea,
 Shining with all his might:
He did his very best to make
 The billows smooth and bright -
And this was odd, because it was
 The middle of the night.

The moon was shining sulkily,
 Because she thought the sun
Had got no business to be there
 After the day was done -
'It's very rude of him,' she said,
 To come and spoil the fun!'' '

Maraja. W.H. Allen, London 1959.

' "O Oysters," said the Carpenter,
 "You've had a pleasant run!
Shall we be trotting home again?"
 But answer came there none -
And this was scarcely odd, because
 They'd eaten every one." '

Sir John Tenniel. Macmillan, London 1872.

'But four young Oysters hurried up,
    All eager for the treat:
Their coats were brushed, their faces washed,
    Their shoes were clean and neat -
And this was odd, because, you know,
    They hadn't any feet.'

Blanche McManus. Mansfield, New York 1899.

Chapter 5
Wool and Water

''"I wish *I* could manage to be glad!'' the Queen said. "Only I never can remember the rule." ''
J. Morton Sale. William Clowes, London 1933.

'suddenly the needles turned into oars in her hands, and she found they were in a little boat, gliding along between banks: so there was nothing for it but to do her best.'
Mervyn Peake. Zephyr Books, Stockholm 1946.

Chapter 6
HUMPTY DUMPTY

'the egg only got larger and larger, and more and more human: when she had come within a few yards of it, she saw that it had eyes and a nose and mouth; and when she had come close to it, she saw clearly that it was HUMPTY DUMPTY himself.'
Philip Gough. The Heirloom Library, London 1949.

'Humpty Dumpty was sitting, with his legs crossed like a Turk, on the top of a high wall - such a narrow one Alice quite wondered how he could keep his balance - and, as his eyes were steadily fixed in the opposite direction, and didn't take the least notice of her, she thought he must be a stuffed figure, after all.'

Edgar B. Thurstan. Juvenile Productions, London.

Chapter 7
The Lion and the Unicorn

Above:
'The King was evidently very uncomfortable at having to sit down between the two great creatures; but there was no other place for him.'
Robert Högfeldt. Jan Forlag, Stockholm 1945.

Left:
'But before Alice could answer him, the drums began. Where the noise came from, she couldn't make out: the air seemed full of it, and it rang through her head till she felt quite deafened.'
Sir John Tenniel. Macmillan, London 1872.

' ''Were you happy in prison, dear child?'' said Haigha. Hatta looked round once more, and this time a tear or two trickled down his cheek; but not a word would he say. ''Speak, ca'n't you!'' Haigha cried impatiently. But Hatta only munched away, and drank some more tea.'
Mervyn Peake. Zephyr Books, Stockholm 1946.

Chapter 8
"It's My Own Invention"

'they began banging away at each other with such fury that Alice got behind a tree to be out of the way of the blows.'
Blanche McManus. Mansfield, New York 1899.

'The Knight looked so solemn about it that Alice did not dare to laugh.'
J. Morton Sale. William Clowes, London 1933.

Chapter 9
QUEEN ALICE

Left:
Mervyn Peake. Zephyr Books, Stockholm 1946.

Right:
"What *am* I to do?'' exclaimed Alice, looking about in great perplexity, as first one round ʜead and then the other, rolled down from her shoulder, and lay like a heavy lump in her lap.'
Robert Högfeldt. Jan Forlag, Stockholm 1945.

' "Well, this is grand!" said Alice. "I never expected I should be a Queen so soon." '
Peter Blake. Screenprint, 1970.

'The leg of mutton got up in the dish and made a little bow to Alice; and Alice returned the bow, not knowing whether to be frightened or amused.'
Peter Newell. Harper, New York 1902.

Chapter 10
SHAKING

'She took her off the table as she spoke,
and shook her backwards and forwards
with all her might.'
Edgar B. Thurstan. Juvenile Productions,
London.

Chapter 11
WAKING

'it really *was* a kitten, after all.'
Sir John Tenniel. Macmillan, London
1872.

Chapter 12
WHICH DREAMED IT?

Maria Barrera. Editorial Bruguera, S.A., Barcelona 1956.

Alice Lidell, c. 1858.

Edith, Lorina and Alice Lidell

Alice Lidell, c. 1859

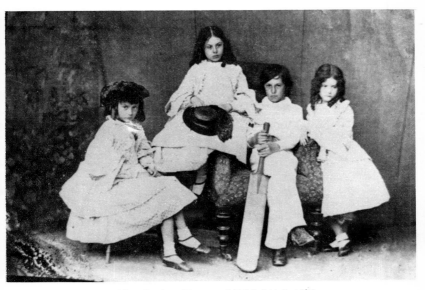

Alice, Lorina, Harry and Edith Lidell, 1859.

Alice Lidell, late 1850s

ALICE IN WONDERLAND

ACCORNERO, V. Murrays, London 1968.
ACKROYD, Winifred. London 1930.
ADAMS, Frank. Oxford University Press, London 1912.
ALLEN, Olive. Edward Arnold, London 1910.
ALPINO, L'. Odhams, London 1966.
APPLETON, Honor C. Harrap, London 1945 and New York.
ATTWELL, Mable Lucie. Raphael Tuck, London 1910 and New York 1910.
BACKHOUSE, G.W. William Collins, London 1951.
BLASCO. Idea Books, Croydon, n.d.
BLUM, Alex A. Gilberton, New York 1948.
BOSWELL, Hilda. William Collins, London 1973.
BOWLEY, Ada. McKay, Philadelphia 1926.
BOWLEY, A.L. Raphael Tuck, London 1921.
BROCK, H.M. Peter Lunn, London, n.d.
BRUCE, Suzanne. Rand, McNally, Chicago 1951.
BUCHANAN, N. W. & R. Chambers, Edinburgh 1909.
CANAIDER. World Distributors, Manchester 1969.
CARROLL, Lewis. *Alice's Adventures Under Ground,* Macmillan, London 1886, New York 1932.
CHAMBERS with GORDON and SPENCER. Graphics International, London; Random House, New York 1968.
CLOKE, Rene. P.R. Gawthorn, London 1943.
COLLES, Dorothy. William Collins, London 1954.
COONEY, F.C. Rand, Chicago 1929.
COOPER, John with David WALSH. Ward Lock, London 1962.
CORY, F.Y. Rand, Chicago 1902.
DALI, Salvador. Random House, New York 1969.
DEMPSTER, Al. Simon & Schuster, New York 1951.
DISNEY, Walt. Disney Productions, California 1948.
DORE, Guy. Hamlyn, London 1970.
DYER, Gil. Foulsham, London 1934.
LeFANU, Brinsley. Stead, London 1907.
FEDERER, A.C. with A.E. JACKSON. U.S.A. 1930.
FOLKARD, Charles. A. & C. Black, London 1929.
FURNISS, Harry. *The World's Great Books,* J.A. Hammerton, London 1909.
GEE, Hugh. Max Parrish, London 1948.
GOODALL, J.S. Blackie, London 1965.
GORDE, Monique. Lito Publishers, Brighton, n.d.
GREENE, Julia with Helen PETTES. Cupples & Leon, New York 1917.
GUTMANN, see PEASE.
HALL, Douglas. Hutchinson, London 1960.
HARDY, E. Stuart. Shaw, London, n.d.
HARGREAVES, Georgina. Dean & Son, London 1974.
HAWES, Walter. W. Scott, London 1908.
HENDERSON, Hume. Reader's Library, London 1928.
HERFORD, O. Ginn, Boston 1917.
HIDALGO. Rylee, London, n.d.
HONEYBOURNE, Rosemary. McClelland & Stewart, Toronto 1969; Purnell, London 1969.
HUEHNERGARTH, John. Winston, New York 1952.
HUDSON, Gwynedd M. Hodder & Stoughton, London 1922; Dodd, New York 1922.
HUTCHINGS. World Distributors, Manchester 1975.

JACKSON, A.E. Henry Frowde: Hodder, New York 1914; Frowde, London 1915.
JARRETT, Dudley. Reader's Library, London 1928.
JOHNSTONE, Janet with Anne GRAHAM. World Distributors, Manchester 1968.
KAY, Gertrude. A. Lippincott, Philadelphia 1923.
KENNEL, Moritz. Elsevier Phaidon, London 1975; Crowell, New York 1975.
KING, Gordon. Purnell, Maidenhead 1976.
KIRK, M.L. Stokes, New York 1904.
LAURENCIN, Marie. Black Sun Press, Paris 1930.
LEE, Winifred A. Charles, London and Glasgow, n.d.
LEONE, Sergio. Golden Pleasure Books, London 1962; New York 1963.
LIVRAGHI and AQUENZA. Odhams, London 1963.
McEUNE, R.E. Milner, London, n.d.
MACIAS, Jose Luis. Hemma, Northampton, n.d.
McKEAN, Emma. C. McLoughlin, Massachusetts 1943.
McMANUS, Blanche. Mansfield, New York 1896; Ward Lock, London 1907.
MARAJA. Grosset & Dunlap, New York 1957; W.H. Allen, London 1958.
MARSH, H.G.C. Educational, London, n.d.
MATULAY, Laszlo. Grosset & Dunlap, New York 1951.
MAYBANK, Thomas G. Routledge, London 1907.
MONRO, Helen. Nelson, London 1932.
MOUNTFORT, Irene. William Collins, London, n.d.
NASH, A.A. Juvenile Productions, London, n.d.
NEILL, John R. Reilly & Lee Co., Chicago 1908.
NEWELL, Peter. Harper, New York 1901.
NEWSOME. Warne, London, n.d.
NORFIELD, Edgar. William Collins, London, n.d.
OVENDEN, Graham. Not yet published.
OVERNELL, Emily. Everett, London 1912.
PEARS, Charles with T.H. ROBINSON. William Collins, London 1908.
PEASE GUTMANN, Bessie. Dodge, New York 1907; Milne, London 1908; J. Coker
    London, n.d.
PETTES, Helen. Cupples, New York 1917.
POGANY, Willy. E.P. Dutton, New York 1929.
RACKHAM, Arthur. William Heinemann, London 1907; Garden City, New York 1907.
RADO, A. W.H. Cornelius, London 1944.
READER, E.K. Philips & Tacey, London, n.d.
RICHARDSON, Agnes. Nelson, London 1920.
RILEY, Harry. Arthur Barron, London 1945.
ROBERTS, K.M. S.W. Partridge, London 1908.
ROBINSON, Charles. Cassell, London 1907 and New York 1907.
ROBINSON, Gordon. Kelley, 1916.
ROBINSON, Normy. Children's Press, London 1963.
ROBINSON, T.H. William Collins, London 1921.
ROLEN, Michael. Brian Basore, Oklahoma 1977.
ROSS, Alice. Nimmo, Hay & Mitchell, Edinburgh 1907.
ROUNTREE, Harry. Nelson, London 1908.
SCHERMELE, Willy. Juvenile Productions, London, n.d.
SEXTON, D.R. J.F. Shaw, London 1933.
SINCLAIR, J.R. National Sunday School Union, London 1909.
SMITH, Jessie. U.S.A., n.d.
SOPER, Eileen. Harrap, London 1947.
SOPER, George. Headley, London 1911; Baker, New York 1911.
SOWERBY, Millicent. Chatto & Windus, London 1907; Duffield, New York 1908.
STADIUM, Art. Hodder & Stoughton, London 1978.
STANLEY, Diana. U.K. 1954.

STANTON, E. Hatton. E.J. Arnold, Leeds, Glasgow and Belfast, n.d.
STEADMAN, Ralph. Dobson, London 1967; Clarkson N. Potter, New York 1973.
TARRANT, Carol. Longman, London 1976.
TARRANT, Margaret. Ward Lock, London 1916.
TENNIEL, Sir John. Macmillan, London 1865; Appleton, New York 1866.
TORREY, Marjorie. Random House, New York 1946; Purnell, London 1964.
TOVEY, R.M. William Collins, London 1938.
VOLKER, Reinhard. Rylee, London, n.d.
WALKER, W.H. John Lane, London 1907 and New York 1907.
WALSH, David. Blackie, London 1954.
WEHR, Julian. n.d.
WOODWARD, Alice. G. Bell, London 1913; Macmillan, New York 1913.

THROUGH THE LOOKING-GLASS
BRIDGEMAN, F. and others. Crowell, New York 1900.
BLAKE, Peter. Not yet published.
CLOKE, Rene. P.R. Gawthorn, London 1950.
COLLINSON, Marjorie. Maxton, New York 1947.
CORY, F.Y. Rand, Chicago 1917.
FULLERTON, Nan. Spring Books, London, n.d.
GEE, Hugh. Max Parrish, London 1950.
HICKLING, P.E. Ward Lock, London, n.d.
HUGHES, Franklin. Cheshire House, New York 1931.
KAY, Gertrude. Lippincott, Philadelphia 1929.
KIRK, M.L. F.A. Stokes, New York 1905.
LEONARD. Golden Pleasure Books, London 1962.
McMANUS, Blanche. Mansfield & Wessels, New York 1899.
MARAJA. W.H. Allen, London 1959; Duell, Sloan & Pearce, New York 1963.
MONRO, H. Nelson, London 1937.
MOUNTFORT, Irene. William Collins, London, n.d.
NEWELL, Peter. Harper, New York 1902.
PEASE GUTMANN, Bessie. Dodge, New York 1909.
PRITTIE, Edwin J. Philadelphia 1929.
RATCLIFF, G.H. Spring House, London, n.d.
ROUNTREE, Harry. U.K. 1928.
STEADMAN, Ralph. McGibbon & Kee, 1972; Clarkson N. Potter, New York 1973.
TENNIEL, Sir John. Macmillan, London 1872; New York 1872.
THURSTAN, Edgar B. Juvenile Productions, London, n.d.

ALICE IN WONDERLAND and THROUGH THE LOOKING-GLASS
ABBOTT, Eleonore P. Jacobs, Philadelphia 1912.
BAYNES, Pauline. Blackie, London 1950.
BLITHE. Studley Press, London 1948.
BRYAN, Brigitte. Classic Press Inc., San Rafael, California 1969.
CARD, Linda. Whitman, Racine, Wisconsin 1945.
CLEMENTS, M.L. Hutchinson, London 1934.
COLLES, Dorothy. William Collins, London 1954.
COLLINSON, Marjorie. Maxton, New York 1947.
COOKE, Donald E. Holt, Rinehart & Winston, New York 1957.
DAVIS. U.S.A. 1910.
DAVIS, J. Watson. A.L. Burt, New York, n.d.
DOHERTY, Dorothy A. Rylee, London, n.d.
GOUGH, Philip. The Heirloom Library, London 1949.
HOGFELDT, Robert. Jan Forlag, Stockholm 1945.
KREDEL, Fritz. U.S.A. n.d.

LEONARD. Golden Pleasure Books, London 1962.
MACKNIGHT, Ninon. Platt & Munk, New York 1937.
McMANUS, Blanche. A. Wessels, New York 1900.
MONRO, Helen. London, n.d.
MORRISS, Patricia. Beaverbrook Newspapers, London, n.d.
MONTFORT, Irene. William Collins, London 1939.
PAFLIN, Roberta. Whitman, Racine, Wisconsin 1955.
PEAKE, Mervyn. Zephyr Books, Stockholm 1946; Allen Wingate, London 1954
PRITTIE, Edwin J. Winston, Philadelphia 1923.
R.G.R. Andrew Dakers, London, n.d.
ROUNTREE, Harry. William Collins, London 1928.
SALE, J. Morton. William Clowes, London 1933.
SCHROEDER, T. Western Publishing Racine, Wisconsin, 1970.
STANLEY, Diana. J.M. Dent, London 1954; E.P. Dutton, New York 1954.
STEVENS, Beatrice. Collier, New York 1903.
TENNIEL, Sir John. Macmillan. London 1887. New York 1881.
THORNE, Jenny. Purnell, Maidenhead 1975.
THURSTAN, Edgar B. Odhams, London, n.d.
VAN HOFSTEN, Hugo. U.S.A. n.d.
WALSH, David and John COOPER. Ward Lock, London 1962.
WATSON, A.H. William Collins, London 1939.
WELLING, Gertrude. Sears, New York 1926.
WIESGARD, Leonard. Harper, New York 1949.
WINTER, Milo. Rand, McNally, Chicago 1916.

Robert Högfeldt, 1945.

Bambini de Carroll, Le. Foto e lettere di L. Carroll a Mary, Alice, Irene, Agnese . . . Franco Maria Ricci editore, Parma 1974.

Bowman, Isa. *The Story of Lewis Carroll,* J.M. Dent, London 1899; Dover, New York 1972.

Burdick, Loraine. *Alice in Wonderland,* Celebrity Doll Club Magazine, Seattle, February 1970.

Catalogue of an Exhibition at Columbia University, Columbia University Press, New York 1932.

Clark, Anne. *Lewis Carroll - a biography,* J.M. Dent, London 1979.

Cohen, Morton N. (ed.) *Lewis Carroll Letters.* Macmillan, London 1979.

Collingwood, Stuart Dodgson. *The Life and Letters of Lewis Carroll,* T. Fisher Unwin, London 1898.

The Lewis Carroll Picture Book, T. Fisher Unwin, London 1899; Dover, New York 1961.

Doyle, Brian. *The Who's Who of Children's Literature.* Hugh Evelyn, London 1968.

Gardner, Martin. Introduction to *The Wasp in a Wig,* Lewis Carroll Society of North American, New York 1977; Macmillan, London 1977.

The Annotated Alice, Clarkson N. Potter, New York 1970; Penguin Books, Harmondsworth 1970.

Gernsheim, Helmut. *Lewis Carroll Photographer,* Max Parrish, London 1949; Dover, New York 1969.

Gilmore, Maeve. *A World Away. A Memoir of Mervyn Peake,* Gollancz, London 1970.

Green, R.L. *The Story of Lewis Carroll, Methuen, London 1949.*

The Diaries of Lewis Carroll, Cassell, London 1953.

Heath, Peter. *The Philosopher's Alice,* St. Martin's Press, New York 1974; Academy Editions, London 1974.

Hudson, Derek. *Lewis Carroll,* Constable, London 1954. New illustrated edition 1976.

Huxley, Francis. *The Raven and the Writing-Desk,* Thames & Hudson, London 1976.

Lennon, Florence Becker. *Victoria Through the Looking-Glass,* Simon & Schuster, New York 1945.

Madan, Falconer (ed.) *Lewis Carroll Centenary Exhibition.* J. & E. Bumpus, London 1932.

Mare, Walter de la. *Lewis Carroll,* Faber & Faber, London 1932.

Mespoulet, Marguerite. *Creators of Wonderland,* Arrow Editions, New York 1934.

Pudney, John. *Lewis Carroll and his World,* Thames & Hudson, London 1976.

Reed, Langford. *The Life of Lewis Carroll,* W. & G. Foyle, London 1932.

Smith, R.D. Hilton. *Alice One Hundred,* Adelphi Book Shop, Victoria B.C., Canada 1966.

Taylor, A.L. *The White Knight,* Oliver & Boyd, London 1952.

Weaver, Warren. *Alice in Many Tongues,* University of Wisconsin Press, Madison U.S.A. 1964.

Williams, S.H. *A Bibliography of the Writings of Lewis Carroll,* The Bookman's Journal, London 1924.

Williams and Madan. *A Handbook of the Literature of the Rev. C.L. Dodgson,* Oxford University Press, London 1931.

Williams and Madan, revised by R.L. Green. *The Lewis Carroll Handbook,* Wm. Dawson, Folkestone 1970, further revised by Denis Crutch, Wm. Dawson, 1979.

Wood, J.P. *The Snark was a Bojum,* Pantheon Books, New York 1966.

INDEX

Bessie Pease Gutmann, 1908.